The Ultimate Pursuit

The Ultimate Pursuit:
A Persian Transmigration

New and Selected Poetry

by Diane Marquart Moore

Border Press
PO Box 3124
Sewanee, TN 37375

borderpress@gmail.com

www.borderpressbooks.com

Border Press
PO Box 3124
Sewanee, Tennessee 37375
borderpress@gmail.com
www.borderpressbooks.com

ISBN: 978-0-9997804-5-9

Library of Congress Control Number: 2019934616

Cover painting by Paul Marquart and drawings by Rose Anne Raphael

Cover design by Victoria I. Sullivan

Printed in the United States

What you seek is seeking you... Rumi

For my Father and Mother, Harold and Dorothy Marquart

ALSO BY DIANE MARQUART MOORE

POETRY

All Love,
Let the Trees Answer
Spring's Kiss
Above the Prairie
Sifting Red Dirt
A Slow Moving Stream
Street Sketches
Corner of Birch Street
Strand of Beads
A Lonely Grandmother
Between Plants and Humans
Night Offices
Departures
In a Convent Garden
Mystical Forest
Everything is Blue
Post Cards From Diddy Wah Diddy
Alchemy
Old Ridges
Rising Water
The Holy Present and Farda
Grandma's Good War
Afternoons in Oaxaca (Las Poesias)
The Book of Uncommon Poetry
Counterpoint
Your Chin Doesn't Want to Marry
Soaring
More Crows
Just Passing Through
Moment Seized

YOUNG ADULTS

Martin and the Last Tribe
Martin Finds His Totem
Flood on the Rio Teche
Sophie's Sojourn in Persia
Kajun Kween
Martin's Quest

ADULT FICTION

Redeemed by Blood
Silence Never Betrays
Chant of Death with Isabel Anders
Goat Man Murder
The Maine Event
Nothing for Free

CHILDREN

The Beast Beelzebufo
The Cajun Express

NON-FICTION

Porch Posts with Janet Faulk-Gonzales
Iran: In A Persian Market
Their Adventurous Will
Live Oak Gardens
Treasures of Avery Island

TABLE OF CONTENTS

INTRODUCTION

I was introduced early to poetry, teething first on *A Child's Garden of Verses* by Robert Louis Stevenson. At eight, while visiting my maternal grandmother in Franklinton, Louisiana, I received "expression lessons" and widened my poetic horizons to include writings by Longfellow and Poe. Meanwhile, my father, who loved wine and song, almost daily strode through my teen years reciting quatrains from the *Rubaiyat of Omar Khayyam,* and I developed an abiding interest in this Persian classic.

After marrying I carried a worn copy of the *Rubaiyat* to Limestone, Maine where my husband had been sent as an Operations Intelligence radar specialist with the U.S. Army. During an illness, isolated by snow and temperatures dipping below zero, I huddled around an oil stove in an old farmhouse and memorized quatrains of the *Rubaiyat* that I can still recite when asked for renditions (which I might add are "seldom events").

Almost twenty years later, my husband, who had become a petroleum engineer for Texaco, received word that we were being sent to Persia (now called Iran), and I felt that the assignment, through some kind of strange synchronicity, could be viewed as a natural follow-up to so many doses of Omar Khayyam's poetry, pre- and post-marriage.

In Ahwaz, Iran, I received a further introduction to Persian poetry — Rumi, Ferdowsi, Sa'Di, Hafez — the greats that Hassan Hosseinipour, the editor of a National Iranian Oil Company publication called the *Yaddash Haftegy,* felt I should read. I began writing articles in English for this newspaper and for the *Daily Iberian* in New Iberia, Louisiana, my home base. Also, when assailed by homesickness, I wrote poetry in a manuscript entitled *When West Meets East,* the title of the first poem I wrote at my rickety tin desk in a room facing the dusty streets of Melli Rah Subdivision and later published by Hosseinipour under the header of "The Poetic Homemaker."

During the two years I lived in Iran, I received a gift of an edition of *The Rubaiyat,* a translation by Edward Fitzgerald and illustrated by the famous miniature artist, Behzad Miniatur, to which I refer when my memory, at 83, falters on some beloved quatrain. I have written three books about my experiences in Persia, the last one a book of poems published in 2009 and have continued to expand my shelves to include many volumes by and about Rumi, another great Persian poet.

Several weeks ago, I went outdoors to get into my car and heard a rooster crowing on a street behind my house, and a phrase from the *Rubaiyat* flashed into my memory: "And as the cock crew…" Every time I stepped outside and heard his daily cries, since he crows throughout the day, the phrase resounded in my mind. Giving that anonymous rooster a Persian identity, I began to write down poems about transmigration that came in a rush, and the writing became *The Ultimate Pursuit,* new poems and selected ones from *Farda,* with apologies to the great lyricists of Persia who gave me the impetus to write this small group of poems.

Diane Marquart Moore
New Iberia, Louisiana
January, 2019

I. NEW POEMS

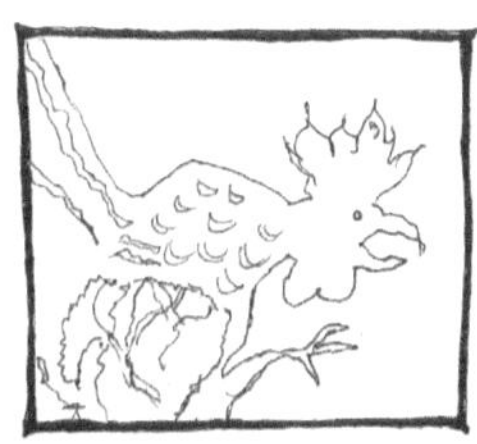

THE LITTLE WHILE WE HAVE TO STAY

A rooster across the coulee
crows into frozen air;
Chicken yards within the city,
off limits, no hens clucking about

so why is he there?
Is he imprisoned for cock fights,
to act as a morning alarm
or to sound out Cajun prophecies –

death for someone known?
All day long deep in trouble
he crows –
dawn, noon

evening, departing light –
like a Benedictine monk
marking the hours.
But he's in a cage

singing the blues:
If I had my way
I'd rip this cage apart,
the earth isn't my home.

I'll find that hen,
sweetly clucking…
waiting in my grave.

MORE LIKELY AN OPERETTA

Lost civilizations
arrive on his wings,
his primitive cry
opens the door

and out of night
he becomes next year's gloom,
willing to be
a caricature of sound

shrill beneath
the red comb,
flaming with inner rage
and never leaving home.

He makes the air waver,
nothing added, nothing needed,
repeating blue notes
on imaginary roads.

A MINIMALIST?

He is alone,
no crowing matches in chorus;
elephant ears edging the coulee
catch every sound

two hours before dawn
when street lights often conflate
unwritten sheet music
in shrill, syncopated rhythms.

He does not hear
his own screams,
nature having gifted him
with built-in ear plugs;

his Phillip Glass symphonies
make us uncomfortable
but like maestro, he can't stop himself
even if he wanted to,

like us, every morning song
reminds us we don't know
what we're doing here
an echo always sounding the same.

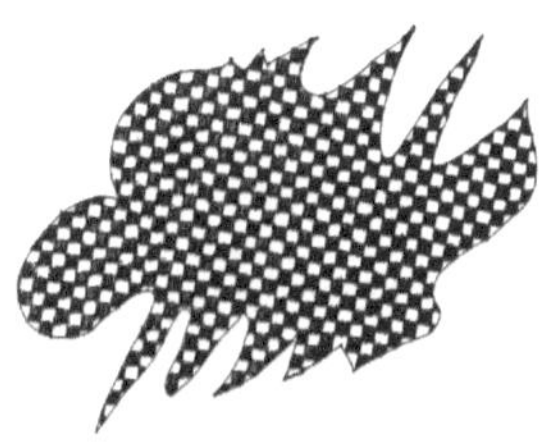

LAMENT

He dreamed of a speckled hen
playing a lute under a tree
laden with a thousand rose blooms

and pointed his beak upward
crowing louder the message
that he knew both heaven and hell

and wondered if an uncaged hen
sang to him how it would be.
Awhile alive? And then

would life become the same again
a senseless nothing
telling him there is no reward?

Whether he believed so or not
he would meet his fate soon,
the shadow lying under a drooping oak.

He would be thrown into the field,
struck down in the dust
without forgiveness

and the moon would look
for him to rise again,
strut in Paradise

without debt,
fulfilled desire, repaid
in blue and gold and red brilliance

for having lived the life
of a helpless creature
readying for another ascent.

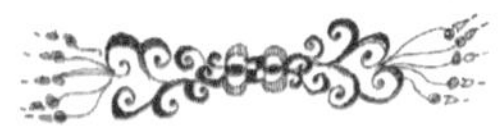

GAME CHANGE

The men took him to a ring
near Eunice, "Fight and die,"
they said, and he was sent

a short while to the Land of the Dead,
re-formed as human life in Persia,
land of ancient cock fights;

becomes a female dancer dressed
in flimsy peignoirs who seduces
drunken men shouting

for taverns to open at dawn
then bringing her to the couches
of their insatiable appetites,

extolling wine, her beauty,
and roses that blossomed and died.
She became the object of nightingales' songs,

holding out her hands to new guests
as if dispensing treasure
to old acquaintances.

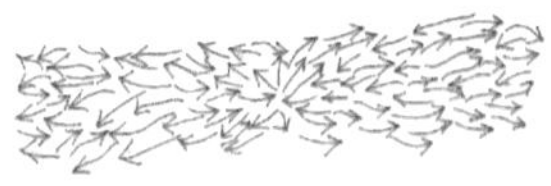

A CLASH OF CYMBALS

And was it not natural to return
to the country of cock fights
whose sages gave us visions of Paradise —
spurs for the Ultimate Pursuit?

Time, the great calamity,
comes in and goes out
the same way.
Aren't men always caging something

and living behind it?
A sword, a stallion pawing at his stall,
the player striking again and again
while two men hammer their drums,

believe they can frighten away
the day of separation.

UNBORN TOMORROW

A lizard flicks his tail
against the dried mud wall,
always a wall surrounding women
that men easily break down;

she, receiving, still plays the lute,
her substance once a shrieking noise,
a rooster remade by the master potter
who gave her this garden —

the Holy Present — to live in,
a gracious trade,
her gowns as green
as the cypress in spring,

the purple desert
outside her window,
a plot of dust
looming like tomorrow

into which she could become again,
a vessel broken into another face,
her veils cast down,
every former Self dying,

untrapped in one life
as she enters into dim awareness
of a mystical variance,
the moment of God.

A VISION OF CYRUS THE GREAT

In Pasargardae,
dwelling place of the Persians,
on a bleached stretch of land
she could hear the hoofbeats

coming out of barren mountains,
quarrelsome sons of Fans
wearing leather helmets, bronze vests
a halo suspended above their heads

marching under Cyrus
uniter of Medes and Persians,
Cyrus, freeing the Jews from Babylon
all for Ahura Mazda, the Creator,

his head rolling at the last
for wanting a kingdom of light
streaming human rights,
justice and peace.

Where and what had she come to?
And why?
Had she regressed to dynasty
and domination again?

A desert breeze blows a dying rose
and her answers into unhearing air:
distillations of wisdom and love
the past had shuttered

now emerge from Cyrus's blue sky
he called Heaven,
a new kingdom on the threshold
of a cooing dove, Persia revived

but phantom figures
throw their shadow on *qalehs**
guarding her, and she turns
with the weather vane of fate.

**walls built around peasant houses*

A PLEA FOR REGENERATION

When the Arabs arrive
blood stains the silken tassels
of her couch, Allah, she cries,
release me to my once form.

God who is in the East,
God who is in the West,
let me become a cleric
or a poet, send me to Qom

or Isfahan, I desire emergence
from a life filling the cup for men;
send me to Bayqara
who loves fighting cocks

where I am *that* again,
crowing lustily,
haunted by zealots and martyrs,
the shadow of God on my face,

peel back the bluest sky
above Isfahan with its colored lights
lighting up half the world
and the turquoise domes of mosques,

a gossamer curtain covering
the king of king's divine personage
exalting a barren plain
where charisma will never die;

or I could be a miniaturist
painting the faces of men
who once embraced me with one hand
and held a cup of wine with the other,

painting them playing polo,
hunting, warring against one another
with brushes made from cat hairs
blue, black, turquoise, gold, and red

leaves, flowers, pots,
old and burdened men,
my lovers' thin forms
crowned with long black hair.

Like Ferdowsi, let me write
another hymn of national glory
like him, I say, "damn the Arab
who forced me to become Muslim;"*

send me to the Timurids:
Rumi, Jami, Mowlani, Hafez
and Omar Kayyam who transcend
the Shia's blind understanding.

**From* The Iranians *by Sandra Mackey*

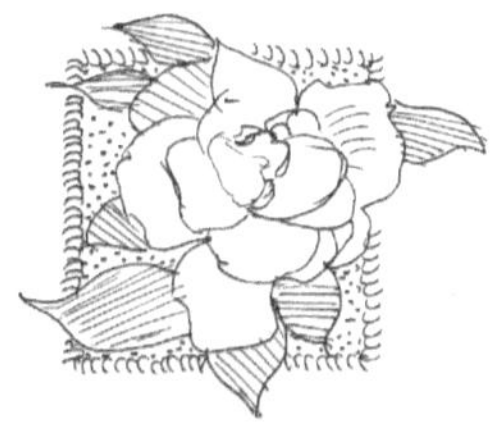

A TEMPORARY SUSPENSION

She lived within *The Gulistan,*
no monarch,
no religion,
God's will manifest

as a Rose Garden.
She was happy within the garden
in words with 75 meanings,
winds blowing over the Persian Gulf

and into the garden:
ranunculus, poppies,
and the rose incarnadine,
poplar trees shading

the candle of the sun,
Secrets of the Unknown
whirling her into deliverance
and the world as One.

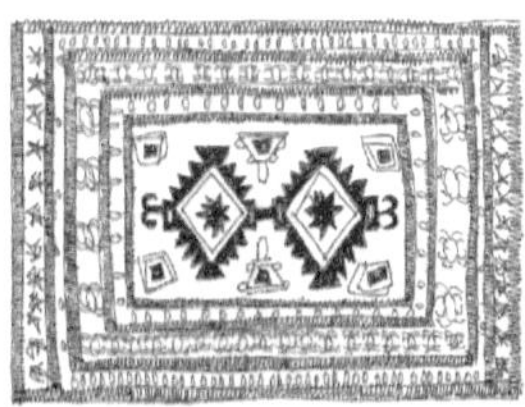

THE SHAHANSHAH

They were fighting again,
this time resisting Pahlavi rule,
and she was made man,
a peasant from Abadan

desperate with longing
who suffered the demise
of the Great Civilization,
the White Revolution;

his memory seeking to elevate
a Past poised as spiritual host
but feeding inward,
caressing yesterday's gods.

Oil, the real monarch,
fomented war in Isfahan,
scantily clad American women
walk through the Friday mosque;

the streets fill with
no place to stand,
Khomeini seeking claim
for religious rectitude

and the Shahanshah
represses Islam,
his mysticism defining
King as God.

Al-e Ahmad,
overcome by orange gas flares,
denounces capitalist parasites,
railing against the western world.

Re-formed as peasant, he realizes
his romantic notions have become
moribund, dreams siphoned off
like the dark film on coastal waters

no longer used to spread
on sores afflicting his tribe
or traded to Arabs plying
the Tiber and Euphrates.

The Brits had come
and opened the earth,
planted their flag in the hearts
of his fellow Baktiara tribesmen,

and he sickens
among nomads without hygiene,
drowns in a lake of oil
that had fueled the Persian Empire.

Ahwaz, once palm trees,
and blood red poppies
becomes fields of land mines beneath
the shallow surface of religious zeal.

Two revolutions defy social justice
and the self-exalted king
departs without his jeweled globe,
Persian soil deep in his pockets.

MESSENGER OF GOD

When the Imam arrives,
he is made god,
his feverish eyes fixed
on a book opening

to pictures of the rooster as woman
lounging on a couch,
pouring wine into chalices
of sensual youths

beside posters of a noose
hanging over the Shahanshah,
a skull on the bloody brim
of his military cap;

Khomeini enthroned, Ruholla shouting,
topples the empires of past centuries,
looks into a mirror, seeing *walayat** not there —
only the cold eyes of a holy war,

a messenger hiding in a black cloak
who delivers wild orations
from a head of roses
attached to a battle jacket.

**ability to perceive mysteries in the* Koran

RETURN

Towers of song in a garden
become Muslim chants,
a Gethsemane in foothills
of the Elburz Mountains.

He is forced to leave this country,
two salt deserts dividing east and west;
highways built in the fall
washed out by flood in spring

falling, falling, the Persians
dark hawks like khalag birds
born to announce winter
sent into the eternal environs —

gray sky straddling
a stretch of sandy earth.
He is loosed from Persia's praying mantis
without exulting triumph,

only the poetry survives,
comes of age every age,
the blood of Persian subtlety —
in this he is transformed again —

dissimilated, synthesized,
brother to the nightingale
returned to a red dawn,
Western promise.

BACK HOME

I.

But would there be an Apocalypse,
slaughter pecking in the backyard,
the tavern closed, church door open?
Now two roosters in the yard,

bloodlines unsullied,
step on each other's shadow,
one quiet in renewed identity,
a stowaway from Persia

who kneels in the dawn,
seeks a cage for all his truths
as if his crowing is a headline
for ideals without stain of corruption.

II.

Later, from his cage
he sees brittle brown leaves
falling, one by one
like his transmigrations,

feels he will not fight again.
When he looks out he sees
a grove of palmetto spikes,
their jade stems, sharp spurs

striking at his peace,
causing a flood of tears
to cover the impulse
toward beginning again,

Where? Why?
So good to have been there,
So good to be here…
now.

No need for valiant jousts
in the Garden of Paradise.
Yet, he sighs for youth,
a sudden impulse toward hope

again enlivened by
the fragrance of spices,
visions of languid couches
cancelling the dull chill of oblivion

and he hears the distant refrain:
Be who you were, Be who you are —
Be the red comb of morning song —
even if dissonant.

II. SELECTED POEMS FROM *FARDA, 2009*

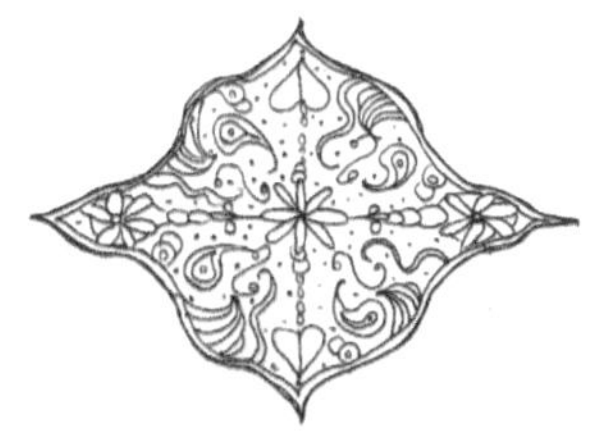

WHEN WEST MEETS EAST

Like mild animals sulking in the white sun
our compass needles heat and run awry;

dust sways a fly on scarlet cherry,
rational cries of deep green birds

fall into the desert sea.

In this strange parchment we dwell
under Eden-like mimosa,

quiet as the old stones
Persians once worshipped,

listening to songs of sand and desolation.
As them, we mild animals

sulk in the white sun,
saying *Enshallah,* Allah wills,

time ticks sand on cracked hogbacks,
softly spilling into Fall oasis.

Farda, the nightingales will sing,
Farda, reach the other half of this world.

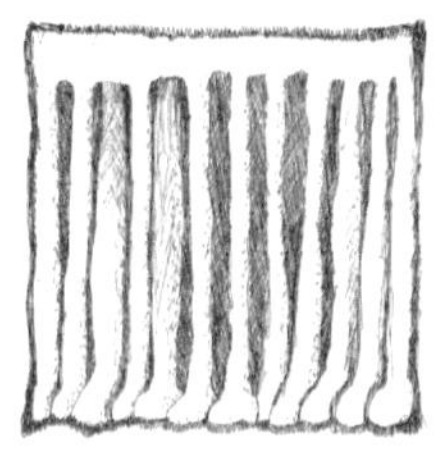

PERSEPOLIS

Persepolis, ruin of the ancient East,
the stones of your palace

gleam like highly polished mirrors
reflecting delicate faces of a vainglorious past;

we stand on the stone of long continuances
of Achaemenian emperors, Darius, Xerxes,

disgraced at the hands of Alexander the Great
who ascended the stone staircase

leading to your dreams;
beyond the wall of date palms

set fire to the state of the free,
the wealth of social accord,

destroying that final bloom,
imperial eastern civilization,

its art now reduced to building missiles,
its architecture to flimsy tents in hot wind,

ghazals about lost battles drifting…
across cloudy mirrors.

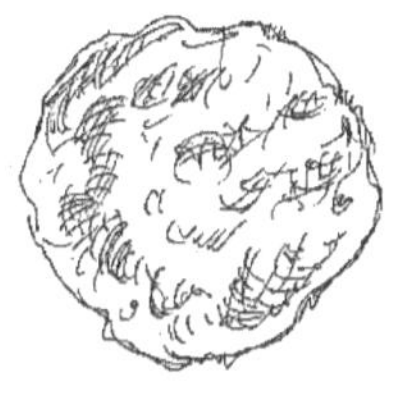

OUR DAILY *NAHN*

At dawn, brown boys, bare chested, emerge,
their black cotton pajama pants loosely strung,

cross the *djube* facing my Melli Rah home,
pitch yellow bricks to one another

and straddle a bed of mortar,
building Persia again.

In the distance gas flares sputter,
tall wicks inflamed by the snarling wind,

Farsi cries run together in racking sound,
shawls and dark beards beg in the bazaar,

chadors flowing down 24 Metre St.

Men come down from rooftops,
asleep to their prayers, bowing to Mecca,

await the flat wheel of bread,
the host slowly peeled, hot and flaky,

gifts from mud ovens on cobbled streets,

chanting *haly mamnum* — for *nahn* —
fragrant and abiding.

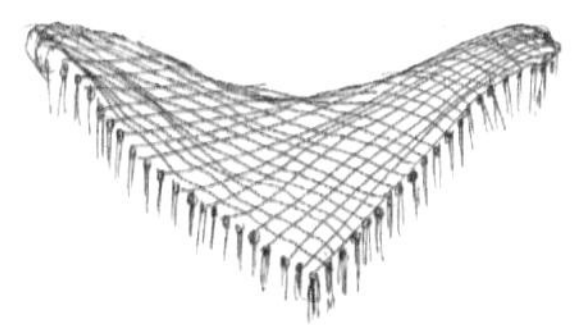

SEARCH FOR THE POWER

Ancient amorphous,
keeper of sacred earth, fire, and water,

weary of seeing dead bodies
exposed on mountain tops until consumed,

you saw the mystery of benign emptiness
lingering beyond Eastern sun,

and charged with electivity of soul,
by your own goodness you created

from the terrors of meaninglessness –
God, a black shawl

begging at our door,
hovering at Kharg Island,

waiting for the Greeks' fine blocks of stone,
the Temple of Poseidon,

crying: *discover me*
until we are made one,

until we are together, sun.

CULTURE SHOCK

If Christ based universe on random suffering,
the blood and terror do not fail us,

we are hungry moths fattened only by fear;
strange martyrs casting oil on bread,

grabbing gold rings in the bazaar,
bowing to the first shopkeeper, Trade.

In darkness, turning, seeking,
finding no inner treaties…

Aliens.

IRAN'S OIL BECOMES NATIONALIZED – 1973

Earthworms do not wriggle
in this ammoniac parchment

where expression runs red,
half mad from sun;

there is no lasting here –
scorpion kingdom, temporal domain;

we have fallen into treeless wastes,
metamorphosed,

tongues darting in reptilian hunger,
tasting, recoiling from the bitter oil,

stirring the dense stream until coins,
burdened with the Shah's nose,

sharply minted,
rise to the surface.

ISABEL

"It is not becoming to humanity that I should be silent when birds chant praises." *The Gulistan* of Sa'Di.

I.

Isabel, a small sparrow in the June wind,
could have launched Columbus

with coy false eyelashes,
one swoop of her wing explains

life moves by her wand
splashing cobalt blue on walls

the color of monotonous deserts,
holding hard grains of time

in tiny hands more eloquent
than the 5,000 words she expresses daily.

Isabel says talk is encroachment;
and it is not,

we are all words linking words,
making new continents of being;

from just such rising sparrows
men were sent voyaging,

forth and return,
to discovery – Isabel – delight.

DUR UNTASH

We travel through salt flats, stretches of sand,
sugar cane fields near Haft Tappeh,

sweet stalks untouched
by the arms of the wind,

standing erect in November warmth.

The road leads through Choga Zombie
to the ruins of Dur Untash,

and I climb to my place as high priest,
a chapel atop the three-story ziggurat,

stories nestling into one another,
53 metres to my pulpit

where I lift my arms in rapture
at the outer edge of today,

asking why am I praising
the god Inshaushinak,

lord of the valley of Ab-I-Diz?

Dur Untash, sun dried yellow brick
preserved for three millennia,

a kingly glory never completed
but three stories sturdily manifest,

as if King Untash believed
the sun would never stop beaming

on brick inscribed with cuneiform,
Untash himself carving on them

names of more than 20 deities
who wave to me and my question

as I stand at the peak
honoring yellow brick in a silent dominion.

This is the remnant of a 13th century vision,
marriage rooms, offertory rooms,

storehouses, eleven temples
waiting for the waving gods to visit,

raise their anthems to a dream realized,
open a gate into the realm of new sun —

the hunting preserve
of great Achaemenid and Sassanid kings…

Paradise.

KHARG

Nothing preserves like the sun that blesses Iran,
and Kharg, its island in the Gulf,

trading post of the ancient Palmyrans,
a place of megalithic tombs, fire temple shrines,

holy places hewn in rock;
the sacred monastery of early Christians,

Nestorian priests, who, in alliance
with their Mazdean brothers, shunned celibacy,

built four rooms for their families,
surrounding homes with walls of stone,

created small patches of arable land
to grow the grape of Eucharistic feasts,

Persian Christians before the persecutions
of two centuries,

worshipping on an island of coral
covered by a crust of stone,

a place that Pliny declared
"sacred to Neptune,"

seamen crossing the Gulf
to raise a shrine for God of the Sea

where Arab pirates discovered their resort home,
lured by pearls brought up near the sandy coast.

But when I flew down to Kharg,
awestruck by the clear aqua blue of the Persian Gulf,

looking for antiquity – Poseidon's temple,
Zoroastrian fire temple, Nestorian monastery,

I found a province of his imperial majesty,
sovereign-owned, supertanker export terminal,

rich vein of crude oil pumping through
pipelines in Gachsaran on the mainland,

an oil jetty guarding ancient religious sites...
new neighborhood of world trade.

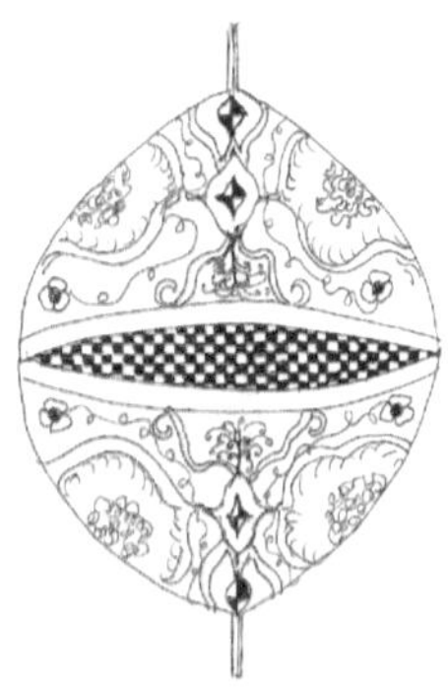

OASIS

Isfahan, half the world in turquoise domes,
vaulted bazaar ceilings,

intricate alleys leading to courtyards
drooping with scarlet rose,

Isfahan, the *Chahar Bagh* where Safavid royalty
promenaded and princes swept by

en route to the *Maidan-I-Shah*
for a round of polo,

a Royal Mosque overlooking
the antics of monarchy,

Islam frowning on half their world.

In the garden of the Hotel Shah Abbas
we strolled beside huge ravens

that dared us to mock the poet's claim
of Isfahan being half the world,

sat in the clear light of Fall,
drinking Tuborg beer,

pondering shaking minarets
and embracing a city of pomp and pleasure.

It was an oasis watered by the *Zayendeh-Rud,*
ancient, life-giving well

planted at the foot of the Zagros,
readying itself for a visit,

Ambassador Kissinger's arrival.
We lifted our glasses to the Shah Abbas,

his empire capital,
to Saggitarius the archer

whose influence hung over the city,
half man, half tiger with snake for tail,

imbedded in bold mosaic everywhere.

Easy for us to settle
into this interlude of half the world,

easy to forget the other half
waiting for us,

the parched fast of Khuzestan's plain.

AT SA'DI'S TOMB

Sa'Di retired on the hill of Pahandez,
orator, poet, pilgrim to Mecca,

twice smashing idols in temples there,
not unlike His Holiness Christ in Jerusalem,

and not unlike St. Francis
he fed the poor, birds, and animals;

yet, was adored by Shiraz princes.
His mausoleum destroyed and built again,

a compound, underneath flowing
spring water as pure as his moral counsel,

pumped to the surface for his rose garden.
Sa'Di, an Isaiah of Persia,

chiding the kings to show justice, equity,
spoke with the heart of a deacon,

serve humankind, he exhorted,
protect the weak and oppressed,

penning 1300 pages of ethical verse,
moral excellence,

studied by Indian and Turkish monarchs,
proclaiming in intrepid lyric,

if we are unaffected by the afflictions of others,
we are not worthy to be called human.

ACKNOWLEDGEMENTS

Thanks to Rose Anne Raphael for wonderful line drawings in the interior of *The Ultimate Pursuit* and for her enthusiastic support of this project;

With respect for my deceased brother Paul's talent and his painting for cover of this volume;

Thanks to Darrell and Karen Bourque who encouraged me to pursue the idea of writing *The Ultimate Pursuit*;

To Victoria I. Sullivan, for constant support and for making certain that all of my poetry appears in print;

To the grand panoply of Persian poets who have inspired me.

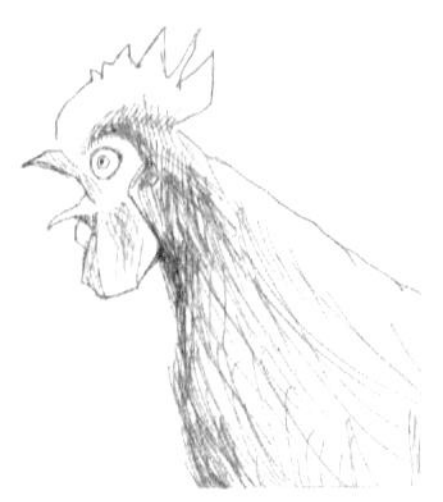

ABOUT THE AUTHOR

Diane Marquart Moore, a writer living in New Iberia, Louisiana and Sewanee, Tennessee (according to the season) spent two years in southern Iran during the 1970s and has published three books about her experiences there. She writes adult fiction and non-fiction, young adult fiction, articles, stories and poems in literary journals; e.g., *American Weave, Trace, Xavier Review, Louisiana Historical Review*, *Pinyon Review*, and other literary journals. She has been an Associate Editor for *Acadiana Lifestyle,* New Iberia, Louisiana, feature writer and columnist for the *Daily Iberian,* and feature writer and book reviewer for *The Yaddash Haftegy,* Ahwaz, Iran. *Sophie's Sojourn in Persia,* a young adult book about Iran was published in 2004 (Publish America, Baltimore, Md.).

In 1995, her young adult book, *Martin's Quest,* (Blue Heron Press, Thibodaux, Louisiana) was adopted as a supplementary Social Studies text in Lafourche and Terrebonne parishes and was a finalist for the Heekins Foundation Award for young adult books. Her books about Avery Island (2001) and Jefferson Island (1991), were among the first guidebooks to these islands of Acadiana (Acadian House Publishing, Lafayette, Louisiana). *Their Adventurous Will,* (Acadiana Press, Lafayette, Louisiana) a volume about memorable Louisiana women was nominated for the Louisiana Library Association's annual award in 1984. A *Chant of Death,* co-authored with Isabel Anders of Sewanee, Tennessee, (Pinyon Publishing, Montrose, Colorado, 2010) features murder in a Louisiana monastery and led to Moore's poetry appearing regularly in *The Pinyon Review*. Border Press, Sewanee, Tennessee have published many of her books of poetry.

She is an accomplished speaker and a former archdeacon of the Episcopal Diocese of Western Louisiana and preaches and serves at St. Mary's Convent during her stay in Sewanee. For the past eleven years, she has published a weekly blog entitled "A Words Worth."

www.ingramcontent.com/pod-product-compliance
Lightning Source LLC
LaVergne TN
LVHW050940080826
845145LV00004B/1348
* 9 7 8 0 9 9 9 7 8 0 4 5 9 *